Great Architects

Written by Jilly Hunt

Contents

Collins

Ancient Egyptians

Architects are people who design buildings. People have been designing buildings for thousands of years.

Some of the oldest buildings can be seen in Egypt. Over 4,500 years ago, the ancient Egyptian **pharaohs** built the first pyramids for their **burial chambers**.

the first step pyramid built in 2630 BCE Egypt

A pyramid shows how powerful a pharaoh was because it would have taken thousands of slaves to build one.

Did you know?

The largest pyramid in the world, the Great Pyramid at Giza, was built for Pharaoh Khufu around 2500 BCE. It is 146 metres high! That's as tall as 35 double-decker buses!

Since the pharaohs of ancient Egypt designed the pyramids, architects have designed buildings for many different uses and in many different styles.

Ancient Greeks

One of the most famous ancient Greek buildings is the Parthenon, in Athens, Greece. It's over 2,450 years old and was designed by two ancient Greek architects called Ictinus and Callicrates. They were asked to build a **temple** to please the Greek goddess of war, Athena.

The Parthenon was built between 447–432 BCE on a **sacred** hilltop called the Acropolis.

The style used in Greek architecture became very popular. This style is called **classical architecture** and it's still used today.

This manor house in England has been designed to look like a Greek temple.

column

Did you know?
The Greeks cleverly designed their columns with a slight bulge in the middle and a narrow top, which tricks the eye into thinking the columns are perfectly straight.

Ancient Romans

Ancient Rome was ruled by powerful emperors over 2,500 years ago. One of Rome's most famous buildings, the Pantheon, was actually designed by an emperor.

The Pantheon is a temple to all gods and was designed by Emperor Hadrian around 118 and 128 CE.

the Pantheon in Rome, Italy

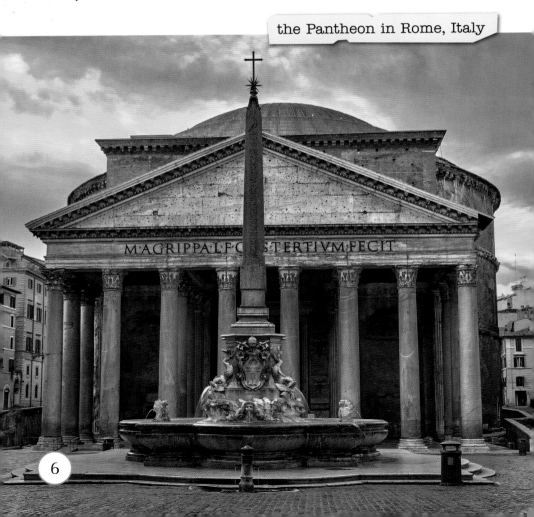

The Pantheon is over 1,800 years old.

Did you know?
The Romans discovered their own form of concrete that allowed them to shape the dome.

The Pantheon is an amazing building because of its size. For hundreds of years, its **dome** was the largest ever built. At the centre of the dome is an opening that lets light flood into the space below.

Brunelleschi's dome

Around 600 years ago in Italy, the builders of Florence's cathedral had a problem. The cathedral, that had been started 100 years earlier, needed a dome to finish it. But they didn't think it was possible to cover the huge space. They held a competition to see who could find a solution.

Filippo Brunelleschi won the competition with his design for an enormous dome that was bigger than any that had been built before. Many people believed the dome would collapse, but it's still there today.

The dome of Florence's cathedral had to be built on the cathedral walls that were already over 54 metres tall. It was completed in 1436.

William Le Baron Jenney

Over 400 years after Brunelleschi's dome, in 1883, architect William Le Baron Jenney designed what is often called the first "skyscraper".

Jenney used materials such as iron and steel to build it. Iron and steel were stronger than bricks and stone so buildings could be built taller and with more windows.

Although it was called a skyscraper, the building was actually only ten **storeys** high.

the first skyscraper in Chicago, USA

Did you know?
Jenney's first skyscraper was **demolished** in 1931 to make way for an even taller skyscraper.

The Field Building is 45 storeys high.

William Le Baron Jenney opened his own architectural firm in 1832. He trained many other architects, including Louis Sullivan who became known as "the father of skyscrapers".

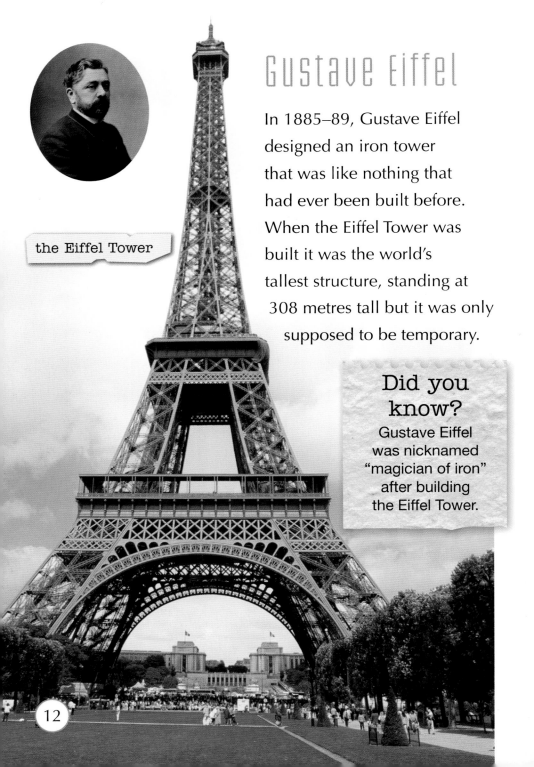

Gustave Eiffel

the Eiffel Tower

In 1885–89, Gustave Eiffel designed an iron tower that was like nothing that had ever been built before. When the Eiffel Tower was built it was the world's tallest structure, standing at 308 metres tall but it was only supposed to be temporary.

Did you know?

Gustave Eiffel was nicknamed "magician of iron" after building the Eiffel Tower.

William Van Alen

In 1929 in New York, the architect William Van Alen was involved in a race against other architects to build the world's tallest building. Van Alen's Chrysler Building only just won because it had a steel spire on top.

The Empire State Building, completed in 1931, is 443 metres high.

The Chrysler Building, completed in 1930, is 320 metres high.

Did you know?

The Chrysler Building was the world's tallest building for four months until the Empire State Building stole the title.

Frank Lloyd Wright

Frank Lloyd Wright is one of America's most famous architects. Wright was born in Wisconsin, USA in 1867. As he was growing up, he dreamt of moving to Chicago where exciting skyscrapers were being built.

In 1887, he did just that and got a job working for an architectural firm in Chicago. He started to develop his own style of architecture known as the Prairie School.

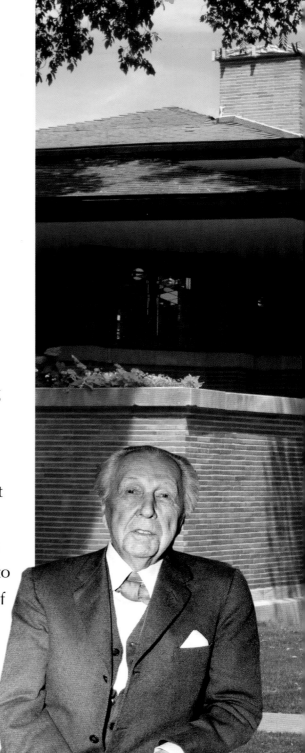

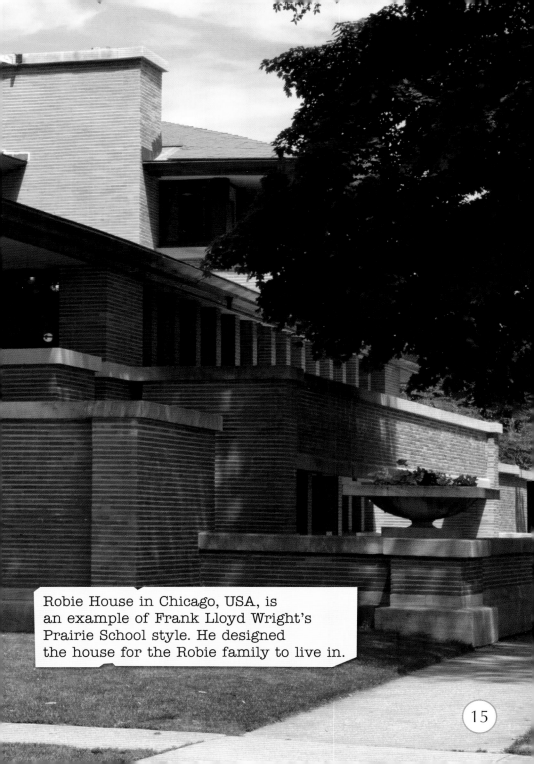

Robie House in Chicago, USA, is
an example of Frank Lloyd Wright's
Prairie School style. He designed
the house for the Robie family to live in.

In 1943, Frank Lloyd Wright was asked to design a building to show the art collection of Solomon R. Guggenheim. He designed a spiral-shaped building that gets bigger as it goes up. Visitors walk up a spiral ramp to view the artwork on display.

The Guggenheim Museum in New York, USA, which opened in 1959, is one of Frank Lloyd Wright's most important buildings.

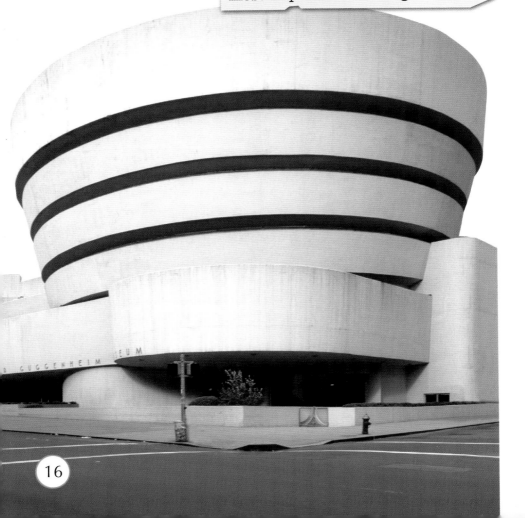

the Guggenheim Museum in Bilbao, Spain

Did you know?
The architect, Frank Gehry, designed a Guggenheim Museum in Bilbao, Spain. It opened in 1997 and is meant for artwork that's too large to show in New York. In 2006, Gehry was asked to design a Guggenheim Museum in Abu Dhabi, which opens in 2017.

Ludwig Mies van der Rohe

Ludwig Mies van der Rohe was born in Germany in 1886. He started working as an architect's **apprentice** when he was just 15 years old. By the time he was 44 years old, he was in charge of an important architecture and design school in Germany.

Mies is known for making his designs look simple and not highly decorated.

Did you know?

Mies thought about every detail of his buildings and even designed the chairs!

In 1937, Ludwig Mies van der Rohe moved to Chicago. Mies created his own style of architecture, using steel and glass to design elegant skyscrapers. His ideas were often copied but not always done as well.

Mies's Seagram Building in New York is covered in **bronze** and glass.

Le Corbusier

Le Corbusier was born Charles-Edouard Jeanneret in 1887 in Switzerland. He was very creative and worked as an **interior designer** and a painter. However, he used his grandfather's name "Le Corbusier" for his architectural work.

Le Corbusier's Villa Savoye was designed and built between 1921–1931 as a family home.

Le Corbusier designed houses with large, open spaces.

Le Corbusier influenced many other architects. He is famous for his modern, concrete buildings that were raised from the ground on stilts.

Le Corbusier's buildings often had roof gardens.

Le Corbusier didn't just design buildings. In 1951, he was asked to design a whole new city, Chandigarh in India. Le Corbusier and his team designed everything in the city from the buildings to the door handles.

Le Corbusier designed many important buildings in Chandigarh, including the **High Court**.

Did you know?

Le Corbusier was worried that when he died all his collections of paintings, writings, notes, albums, travel diaries and even his buildings might be destroyed. He wanted all these items to be shared so he created a **foundation** to look after his work.

Le Corbusier died suddenly while swimming in 1965.

Today's skyscrapers

Throughout history, people have wanted to create the world's tallest building. In 2010, the Burj Khalifa in Dubai became the world's tallest building. It was designed by the Chicago-based architects, Skidmore, Owings and Merrill with Adrian Smith.

The Burj Khalifa is over 828 metres tall and also holds the record for the highest building that people live in.

Before building the Burj Khalifa, the designers carried out tests to see what effect the wind would have on such a tall building. They needed to make sure the design was safe.

Did you know?

One of architect Adrian Smith's latest projects is the world's next tallest building. Kingdom Tower in Jeddah, Saudi Arabia, is due to be finished in 2018 and will become the world's first kilometre-high skyscraper!

Today's influential architects

Many of today's influential architects use their understanding of materials and technology to design some amazing buildings.

Zaha Hadid's design for the **aquatics centre** for the London Olympics looks like a curving wave of water. Local school children have said it's like swimming in a spaceship!

Zaha Hadid was the first woman to be awarded the **RIBA** Gold Medal for architecture.

Zaha Hadid is famous for using curves in her designs.

Japanese architect, Shigeru Ban, uses paper and cardboard to create buildings. He uses glue to strengthen huge cardboard tubes so they can be used as columns and walls. Buildings made from paper and cardboard can be built very quickly. This can be very useful after a **natural disaster**.

Some of today's architects are even designing **spaceports** that will help take people into space!

Ban helped people in Haiti after a terrible earthquake destroyed their homes in 2010.

Glossary

apprentice	person learning how to do a job
aquatics centre	building where people can swim, dive or play some water sports
bronze	metal material with a brownish colour
burial chambers	places where people are buried
classical architecture	style of buildings used by the Greeks and Romans
demolished	knocked down
dome	circular roof
foundation	charity that looks after a particular thing
High Court	court of law
interior designer	person who designs the look of the inside of a building
natural disaster	an event such as an earthquake, hurricane or volcanic eruption
pharaohs	Egyptian kings
RIBA	Royal Institute of British Architects
sacred	holy
spaceports	places like an airport where spacecraft are launched
storeys	floors or levels in a building
temple	building where people go to worship

Index

Timeline of great architects

1436 CE
Brunelleschi's dome for Florence Cathedral was completed.

around 2630 BCE
Egypt's first step pyramid was built.

1883
William Le Baron Jenney designed the first "skyscraper".

118–128 CE
The Pantheon was built by the Roman Emperor Hadrian.

1951
Le Corbusier asked to design the city of Chandigarh, India.

1930
Chrysler Building becomes the world's tallest building.

1997
Guggenheim Museum, Bilbao, Spain opens.

1931
Empire State Building becomes the world's tallest building.

1959
Guggenheim Museum, New York, USA, opens.

2010
Burj Khalifa, Dubai becomes the world's tallest building.

Ideas for reading

Written by Clare Dowdall, PhD
Lecturer and Primary Literary Consultant

Reading objectives:
- retrieve and record information from non-fiction
- read books that are structured in different ways
- discuss their understanding and explain the meaning of words in context
- identify main ideas drawn from more than one paragraph and summarise ideas

Spoken language objectives:
- give well-structured descriptions, explanations and narratives for different purposes

Curriculum links:
- Design and technology: design and make
- History: achievements of the earliest civilisations

Resources: ICT, paper and pencils.

Build a context for reading

- Ask children to describe the most amazing building that they have been in or seen. Model with an example of your own and show a picture from a holiday or trip.
- Look at the front and back covers of the book. Read the title *Great Architects* together and help children with decoding this word. Discuss what architects do and what skills they need.
- Read the blurb aloud together. Ask children to make a list of the oldest and most amazing buildings that have been designed by architects.

Understand and apply reading strategies

- Look at the contents page. Ask children to discuss how the contents are organised. Introduce the idea of chronological order as an organisational device. Read through the contents, helping children to decode unusual vocabulary.